I0821023

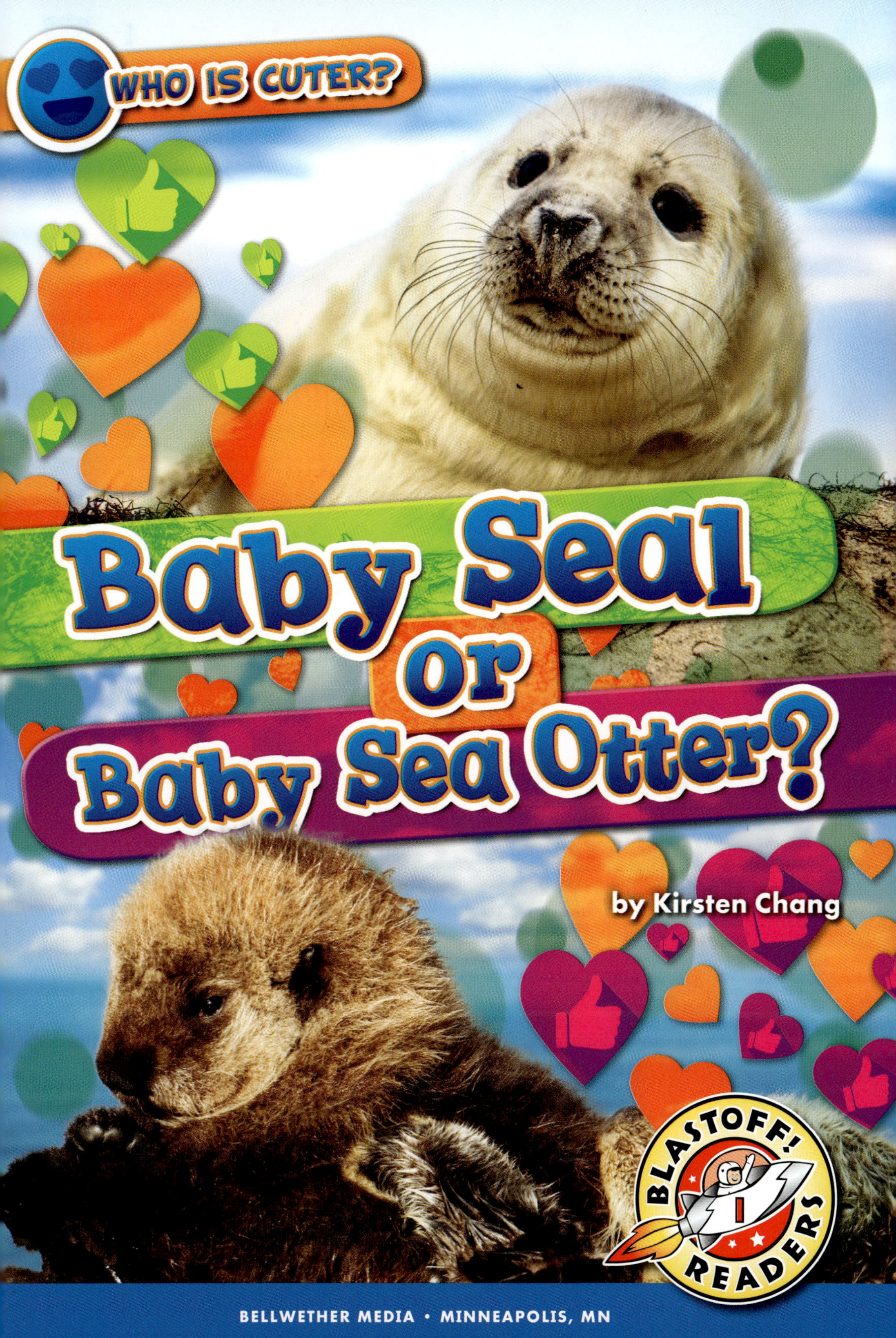
WHO IS CUTER?
Baby Seal
or
Baby Sea Otter?
by Kirsten Chang
BLASTOFF! READERS
1
BELLWETHER MEDIA • MINNEAPOLIS, MN

Blastoff! Readers are carefully developed by literacy experts to build reading stamina and move students toward fluency by combining standards-based content with developmentally appropriate text.

Level 1 provides the most support through repetition of high-frequency words, light text, predictable sentence patterns, and strong visual support.

Level 2 offers early readers a bit more challenge through varied sentences, increased text load, and text-supportive special features.

Level 3 advances early-fluent readers toward fluency through increased text load, less reliance on photos, advancing concepts, longer sentences, and more complex special features.

Reading Level

Grade K

Grades 1–3

Grade 4

This edition first published in 2026 by Bellwether Media, Inc.

Library of Congress Cataloging-in-Publication Data

LC record for Baby Seal or Baby Sea Otter? available at: https://lccn.loc.gov/2025003201

Editor: Rachael Barnes Designer: Brittany McIntosh

Printed in the United States of America, North Mankato, MN.

Table of Contents

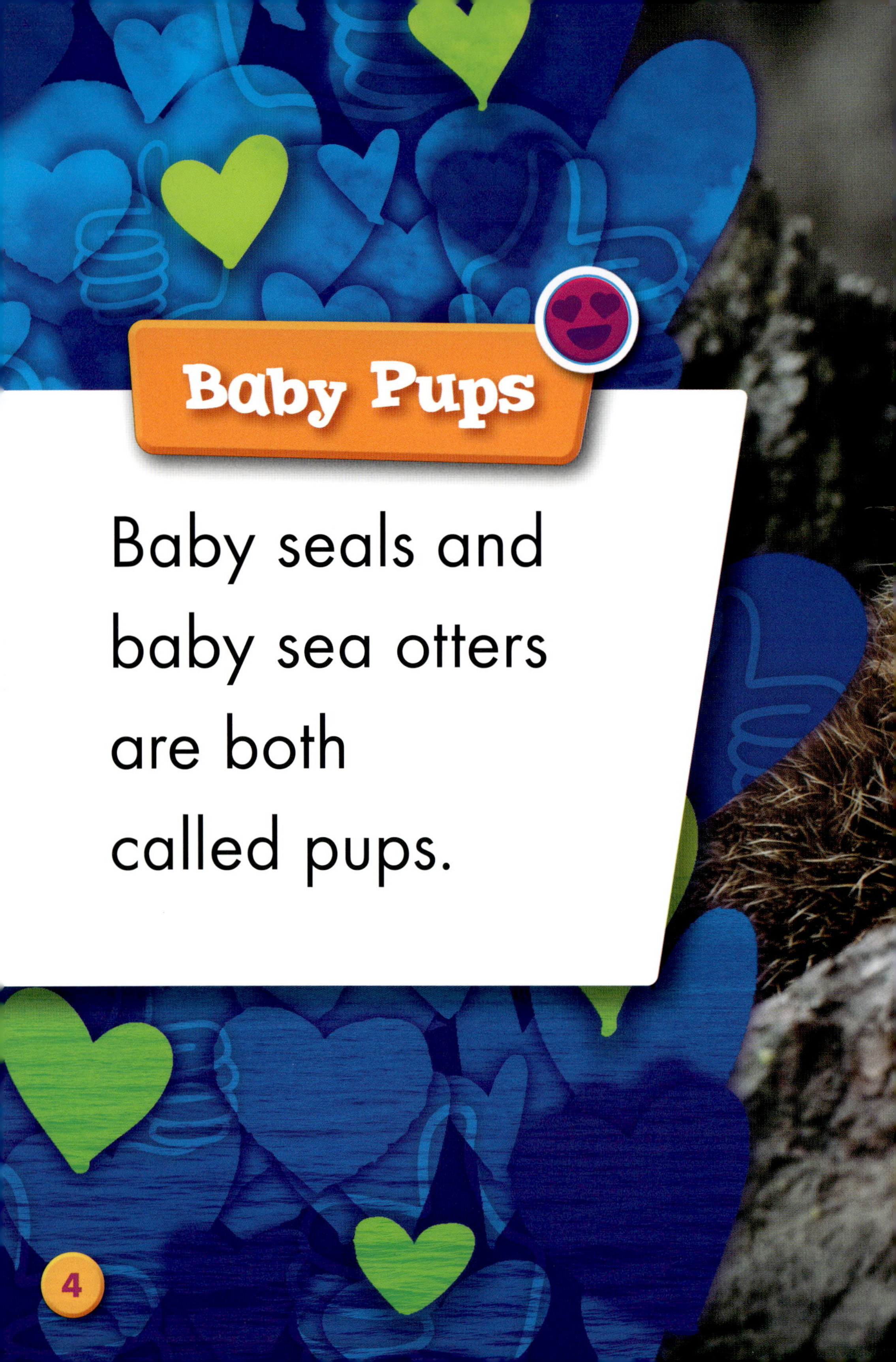

Baby Pups

Baby seals and baby sea otters are both called pups.

sea otter pup
seal pup

These cute babies
have **whiskers**.
They swim with mom!

whiskers

Flippers and Paws

Most seal pups are born with fluffy white **coats**. Sea otter pups have thick brown fur.

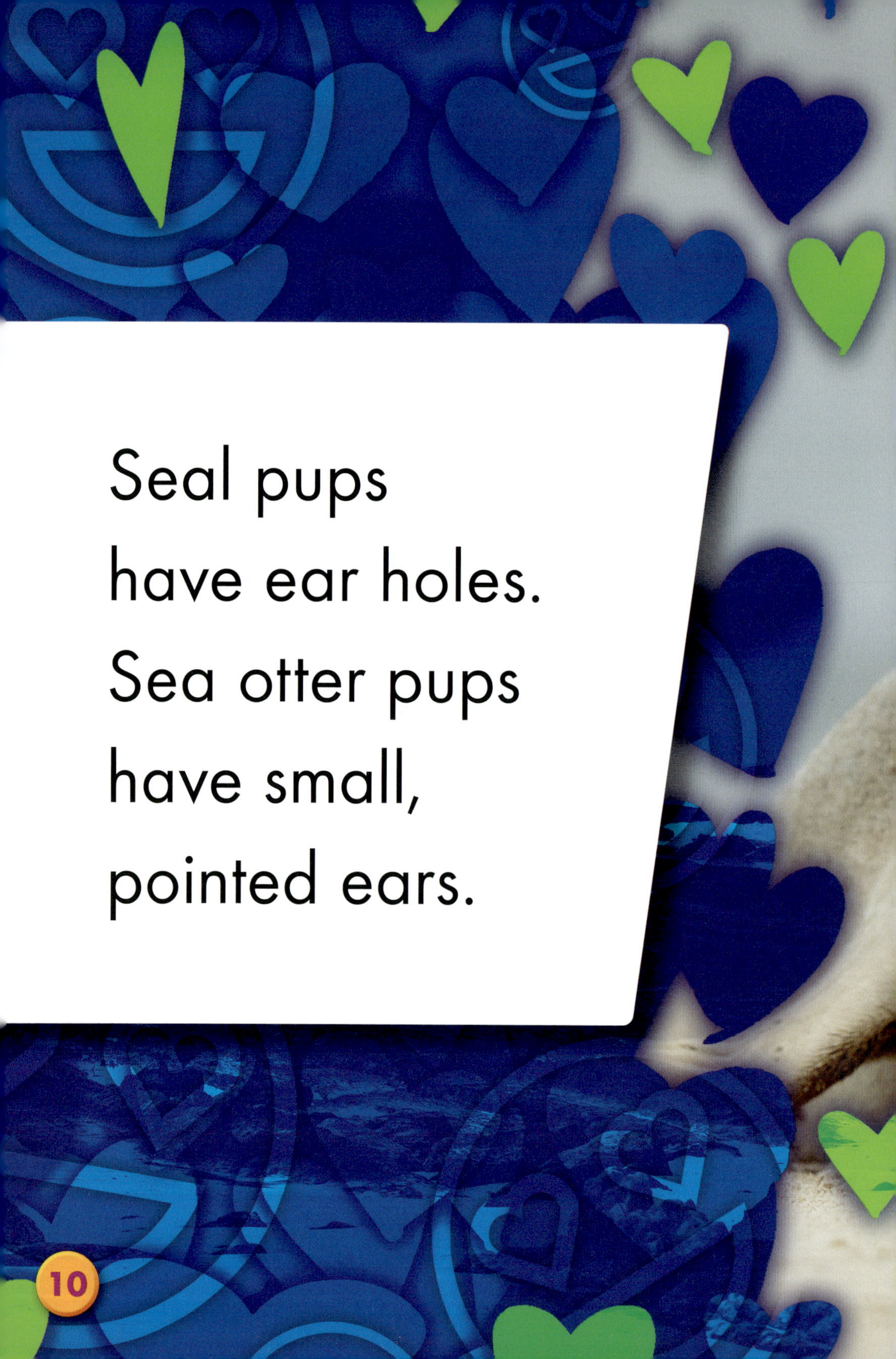

Seal pups
have ear holes.
Sea otter pups
have small,
pointed ears.

ear
hole

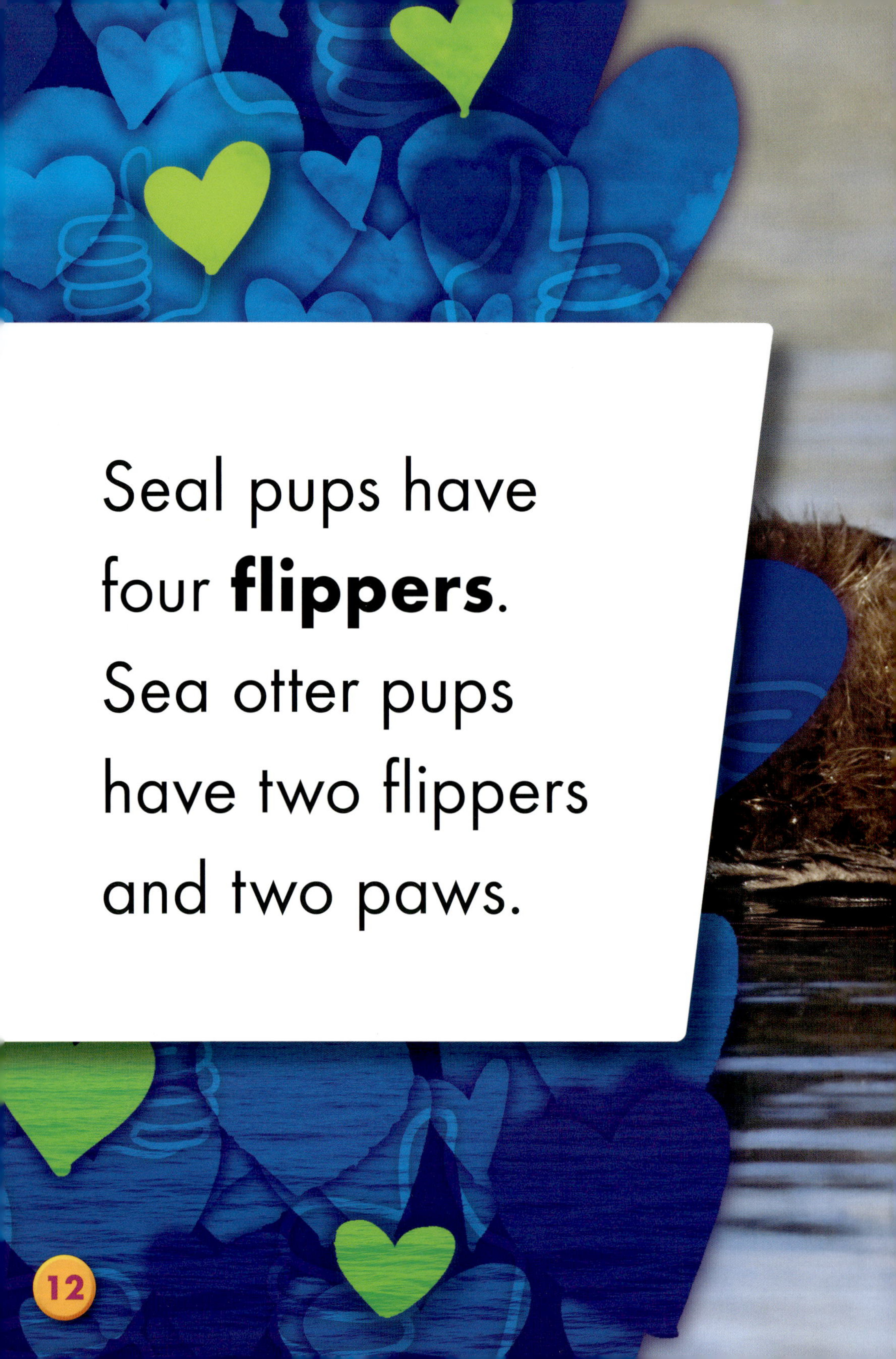

Seal pups have four **flippers**. Sea otter pups have two flippers and two paws.

paws
flipper

Swim and Sleep

Newborn seal pups can **dive**. Newborn sea otter pups cannot. They float!

seal pup
diving

Flippers help
seal pups swim fast!
Sea otter pups use
tools with their paws.

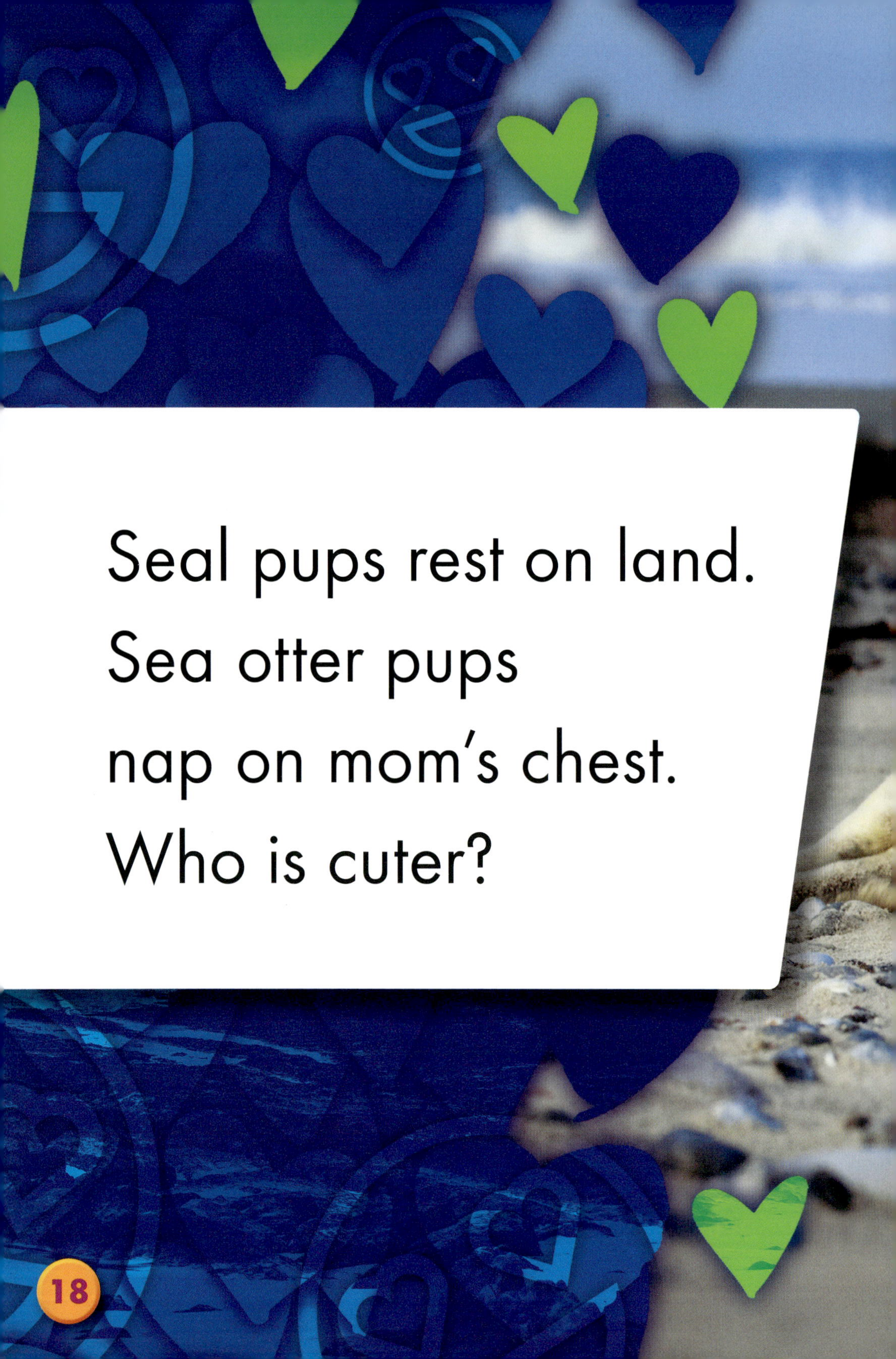

Seal pups rest on land.
Sea otter pups
nap on mom's chest.
Who is cuter?

Who Is Cuter?
ear holes
four flippers
fluffy white coats
Baby Seal
dives
swims fast
rests on land

two flippers
and two paws
Who is your pick?
Vote at
BellwetherMedia.com
small,
pointed
ears
thick
brown fur
Baby Sea Otter
floats
uses tools
naps
on mom's
chest

Glossary

coats

the hair or fur covering some animals

newborn

just born

dive

to move down headfirst into water

whiskers

long, stiff hairs that grow near an animal's mouth

flippers

flat body parts that animals use to swim

To Learn More

AT THE LIBRARY

Boothroyd, Jennifer. *Baby Seals.* Minneapolis, Minn.: Bearport Publishing Company, 2021.

Morlock, Rachael. *Baby Ocean Animals.* Buffalo, N.Y.: PowerKids Press, 2025.

Pringle, Laurence. *The Secret Life of the Sea Otter.* New York, N.Y.: Boyds Mills Press, 2022.

ON THE WEB

FACTSURFER

Factsurfer.com gives you a safe, fun way to find more information.

1. Go to www.factsurfer.com.
2. Enter "baby seal or baby sea otter" into the search box and click .
3. Select your book cover to see a list of related content.

Index

The images in this book are reproduced through the courtesy of: Nicram Sabod, front cover (seal), p. 22 (newborn); Design Pics Inc/ Alamy, front cover (sea otter), pp. 11 (sea otter), 13 (sea otter), 19 (sea otter); Danny Green/ Nature Picture Library, p. 3 (top); GlobalP, p. 3 (bottom); Michael Quinton/ Minden Pictures/ SuperStock, p. 5 (sea otter); Robert Haasmann, p. 5 (seal); Arthur Morris/ Getty Images, p. 7 (sea otter); M. Watsonantheo, pp. 7 (seal), 9 (seal), 22 (flippers); Suzi Eszterhas, p. 9 (sea otter); Lea Scaddan/ Getty Images, p. 11 (seal); emka74, p. 13 (seal); David A Litman, p. 15 (sea otter); Nature Picture Library/ Alamy, p. 15 (seal); Mike Clark/ Alamy, p. 17 (seal); Minden Pictures/ SuperStock, p. 17 (sea otter); blickwinkel/ Alamy, p. 19 (seal); Arterra Picture Library/ Alamy, p. 20; Olga Kamenskaya/ Nature Picture Library, p. 20 (bottom left); Handmade Pictures/ Alamy, p. 20 (bottom center); Roberta Olenick/ SuperStock, p. 20 (bottom right); Chase Dekker, p. 21; Richard Mittleman/ Gon2Foto/ Alamy, p. 21 (bottom left, bottom right); ROBERT67, p. 21 (bottom center); Gerrit Vyn/ Nature Picture Library, p. 22 (coats); Doug Allan/ Nature Picture Library, p. 22 (dive); Vladimir Melnik, p. 22 (whiskers).